CEA

Music for Piano

Favourite Classics
made playable

Air from Suite No 3 in D	Bach
Arrival of the Queen of Sheba	Handel
Jesu, Joy of Man's Desiring	Bach
Jupiter from the Planets	Holst
Largo	Handel
O for the Wings of a Dove	Mendelssohn
The Swan	Saint-Saëns
Waltz from Swan Lake	Tchaikovsky

Arrangements by
Colin Hand and Alan Ridout

Kevin
Mayhew

We hope you enjoy *Favourite Classics Made Playable*.
Further copies are available from your local music shop.

In case of difficulty, please contact the publisher direct:

The Sales Department
KEVIN MAYHEW LTD
Rattlesden
Bury St Edmunds
Suffolk IP30 0SZ

Phone 01449 737978
Fax 01449 737834

Please ask for our complete catalogue of outstanding Instrumental Music.

Front Cover: *The Year's at the Spring, all's right with the World*
by Sir Lawrence Alma-Tadema (1836-1912). Private Collection.
Reproduced by kind permission of Bridgeman Art Library, London.

Cover designed by Juliette Clarke and Graham Johnstone.
Picture Research: Jane Rayson

First published in Great Britain in 1995 by Kevin Mayhew Ltd

ISBN 0 86209 652 9
Catalogue No: 3611153

All or part of these pieces have been arranged by Colin Hand
and Alan Ridout and are the copyright of Kevin Mayhew Ltd.

Printed and bound in Great Britain

Contents

JUPITER from 'The Planets'

Gustav Holst (1874 - 1934)

5

ARRIVAL OF THE QUEEN OF SHEBA

George Frideric Handel (1685 - 1759)

LARGO

George Frideric Handel (1685 - 1759)

AIR from Suite No. 3 in D

Johann Sebastian Bach (1685 - 1750)

THE SWAN from 'Carnival of the Animals'

Camille Saint-Saëns (1835 - 1921)

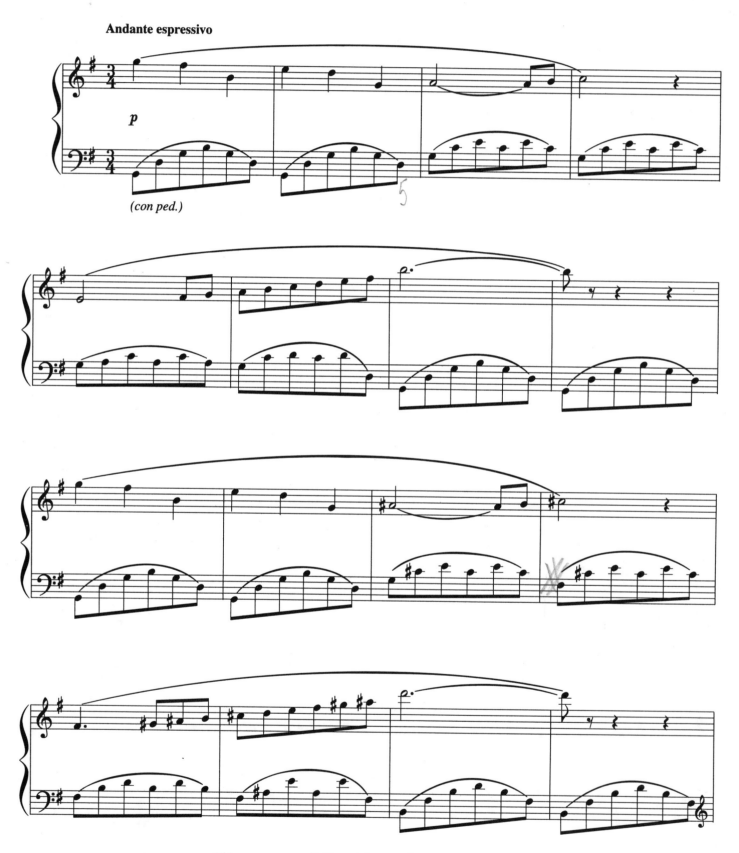

15

WALTZ from 'Swan Lake'

Peter Ilyich Tchaikovsky (1840 - 1893)

19

O FOR THE WINGS OF A DOVE

Felix Mendelssohn (1809 - 1847)

JESU, JOY OF MAN'S DESIRING

Johann Sebastian Bach (1685 - 1750)